ARUBA

The Official Travel Guide

Table of Contents

Introduction

Popular with North Americans (and pretty much the world) wanting to escape biting winters, Aruba is one of Southern Caribbean's most visited island. What makes it so glorious? Everything from stretches of immaculate, white sand beaches to affordable all-inclusive resorts to hip cities (where visitors can enjoy leisurely strolls) draws people to this constituent county of the Kingdom of Netherlands.

There's a lot more to Aruba than its swish resorts too. It houses rough, sun swept views, isolated beaches, shipwrecks (watch out for a couple of airplane wrecks too) and thrilling hiking paths. Plus, who can resist snorkeling and deep sea diving in Aruba's crystal clear sapphire waters. Its beaches also near perfect winds for adventure packed kiteboarding and windsurfing.

This makes the island idea for everyone from lazy beach loungers to outdoor enthusiasts craving adventure. Little wonder then that it enjoys the highest number of repeat visitors among all Caribbean Islands.

Aruba encompasses 32 kilometers from its northwestern to southwestern tip and around 10 kilometers in width. It combines with Bonaire and Curacao to form the ABC Islands trilogy. Together with other Dutch island territories, it is referred to as the Dutch Caribbean.

Aruba is a Lesser Antilles (series of islands forming an arc from northeast South American coast to Puerto Rico) island nestled miles away from the Venezuela coast in Southern Caribbean. On clear, sunny days, one can see glimpses of Venezuela from the south-east region of Aruba. Other islands that are a part of the Lesser Antilles include Saint Martin, Bonaire, Barbados, Curacao, Virgin Islands, Grenada, Trinidad and Tobago and Guadeloupe.

Islands nestled to Venezuela's north coast are referred to as the Leeward Antilles, which Aruba forms a part of along with Bonaire, Curacao along with a few Venezuelan islands like Margarita Island.

Cruise ships descend on this sun and sand draped island weekly, while more than 150 flights from different

North America, South American, England and Netherland cities ply to and from Aruba daily.

Aruba has the maximum number of sunny days across all Caribbean islands. Nestled under the hurricane belt, Aruba features 82-degree days throughout the year with reduced humidity and rejuvenating winds, which makes it one of the most sought after year-round Caribbean hotspots. Yes, any time is actually a good time to visit this stunner of an island!

There are adventure activities, lush national parks, food, shopping, city tours, and much more that make Aruba the obvious choice for visitors from all around the world seeking their fix of sand and sunshine. It also has a distinctly languid pace (which I truly loved) that makes it so relaxing and dreamy.

The Dutch Caribbean Island is an endearing mélange of wilderness, cacti, surfs, casino, Dutch culture and the pleasant Papiamento language. Travelers throng to Aruba to savor its pristine beaches, mesmerizing rugged landscape, swish all-inclusive resorts and a bunch of national parks (the most captivating one being Arikok National Park with its divi-divi trees, erstwhile goldmines and cacti filled landscape). You will find plenty of gambling options in Oranjestad, where visitors can tuck into exceptionally good continental fare and local treats. Shop for crafts and pieces of Delft pottery in addition to plenty of other local artifacts.

Let me give you an interesting peek into what Aruba has in store for you. Here are some experiences you shouldn't miss

- Enjoy hiking, cave exploring and road tripping within Arikok National Park

- Snorkel or day cruise on the azure Caribbean waters.

- Stroll into the vibrantly colored bars, streets, and shops of Oranjestad.

- Experience the ivory white sands of idyllic Eagle Beach.

- Enjoy a glimpse into the island's fascinating past at the Aruba Historical Museum.

Chapter 1
History, Climate, Moving Around and Culture

History of Aruba

Aruba's initial inhabitants were believed to be the Caquetio Amerindians (of the Arawak tribe) who moved here from Venezuela to flee from Carib attacks. The earliest recorded communities here go back to 1000 AD. Since sea travel was particularly challenging owing to dangerous currents, much of the Caquetio settlements thrived within the South American mainland.

It was not until the summer of 1499 that European's got a whiff of the existence of Aruba following the expeditions of Amerigo Vespucci and Alonso de Ojeda. The explorers described it as the "island of giants" (inspiration for Gulliver's travels?) owing to the tall statue of native Caquetios in comparison to Europeans.

When the explorer duo returned to Spain, their tales about the azure island piqued interest in it. Owing to its reduced rainfall density, the island wasn't considered a desirable destination for plantation, finance or even the era's prevalent slave trade. Until now, gold reserves hadn't been discovered.

Spain colonized Aruba for more than 100 years. In 1508, Alonso de Ojeda was appointed as the first

Governor of Aruba. Another Spain appointed governor in Aruba was Juan Martinez de Ampies. The governor was also awarded the right to repopulate Aruba.

While the Netherlands claimed Aruba in 1636, Dutch statues are applicable here since as early as 1629. It was officially under the Dutch rule only post 1636. The Dutch island was a part of the Dutch West India Company as "New Netherland and Curacao" until 1664. The Dutch government appointed an Irishman as Aruba's commander.

Arawaks were left to graze livestock and take to farming, while the Dutch took control of Aruba 135 years posts its Spanish rule. The island was strategically used for sourcing meat and other possessions that the Caribbean's rich natural resources offered.

Come Napoleonic wars, and the ambitious British Empire took complete control of Aruba from 1799 to 1802 and 1804 to 1816. However, it was eventually handed back to Dutch. During the World War II, Aruba's oil resources came under the rule of the Dutch government, which was in exile in London then. Aruba supplied oil to British forces and their war allies.

Aruba island's first constitution for its status apart to be an autonomous state (within Kingdom of Netherlands) was presented in August 1947. It was in 1954 that the Charter of the Kingdom of the Netherlands was set-up, offering a clear structure for the equation between Aruba and the Netherlands.

At a 1972 Suriname conference, an Aruba politician proposed the plan for sui generis Dutch Commonwealth of four states, including Aruba, Suriname, the Netherlands Antilles and the Netherlands, each having its distinct nationality. A referendum was proposed for people of Aruba to choose between total independence and a full autonomous rule under the Dutch Crown.

Croes strived for preparing and educating Aruba citizens about independence. In 1976, a committee chose the island's anthem and national flag as sovereignty symbols. In 1977, during the Referendum for Self Determination held with United Nations' support, about 82 percent of voters voted in favor of independence.

In 1983, the Kingdom drafted an official agreement with Aruba for its independence, broken down into several phases for gradually increasing its autonomy. A constitution was drafted by Aruba in 1985, which was unanimously accepted. On January 1, 1986, Aruba seceded from Netherlands Antilles and officially become a nation of the Kingdom of Netherlands. Though complete independence from the Kingdom of Netherlands was initially planned in 1996, it was indefinitely postponed in 1990 at the Hague convention on the request of the Prime Minister of Aruba.

The article for Aruba's full independence was withdrawn in 1995, though it can be revived following a future referendum.

Though Aruba's official languages are Papiamento and Dutch, Spanish and English are extensively spoken throughout the island, making it ideal for tourists from all around the world.

Aruba Weather

It is a sort of joke among locals here, they do not need any weather forecast because warm and sunshine is nothing out of the ordinary here. With an average rainfall of lower than 20 inches/annually, Aruba's daytime temperatures average at 27 degrees Celsius. Since it is strategically located out of the hurricane belt, it is pleasantly cool and features perfect trade winds, which makes Aruba one of the Caribbean's most moderate weather islands.

The difference in the island's average day and night temperatures is a mere 3.6 degrees, thus making it pleasantly temperate for visitors. Rainfall occurs as sporadic showers between Novembers to December.

When is the best time to visit Aruba?

The best time to visit Aruba is from April to mid-August when the island is not ridiculously priced. There is reduced tropical storm threat as the Aruba sits out of the treacherous Hurricane belt. The weather conditions are perfect from January to March. However, since it is the peak tourist season, prices can be ridiculously high (up to$ 900-1000 per night at the glitzy resorts). Rainfall is low, and temperatures remain pleasantly moderate throughout the day and night.

If you are looking for favorable weather conditions, minus a hefty price tag, plan a trip from April to August. The region anyway features year-round sunshine and temperate weather, which means there really is not much of variance in the climate throughout the year. Though temperatures tend to be on the higher end of the spectrum during this time, Aruba's winds and dry weather prevents it from turning sticky and humid.

From October it gets slightly sultrier, even though the trade winds foil the heart from turning unbearable. Rainfall in Aruba is again moderate from October to December and can go right up to February. Since it is located out of the hurricane belt, it does not witness extended rainfall. Aruba's average year-round temperature is 28 degrees Celsius. Also, the primarily dry climate is suitable for vegetation growth.

Trade winds are constantly blowing, while Aruba's east coast is impacted by powerful sea currents. The island's southern and western coastal belts are more protected and comprise of isolated sandy beaches. Though Aruba is located outside the tropical hurricane belt, hurricanes cannot be completely ruled out. There is still a thin possibility of a hurricane hitting Aruba's coast as it happened IN September 2007 with Hurricane Felix.

The trip can also be planned around one of the several events hosted by Aruba, including the world-famous Carnival that is held annually between January and March. The vibrant and bustling event is spread across several weeks for revelers to enjoy everything from larger than life parades to contests to endless dance and music.

Many visitors own timeshares in Aruba and tend to check out after short weekend trips, which means that the airport tends to be crowded on weekends. If you plan to travel from Aruba during weekends, ensure that you reach the airport at least 3-4 hours before departure.

Geography

Aruba's north coast is a rough terrain comprising different types of vegetation, rough paths, and sand dunes. Sea currents are stronger in the Northern coast compared to Aruba's southern and western coast, and swimming on the northern coast beaches is not recommended. Aruba's most frequented sites like Natural Bridge, California Lighthouse, Natural Pool and Alto Vista Chapel are housed on Aruba's northern coast.

The island's southern coast houses Savaneta, Aruba's oldest town. It is also here that Aruba's second largest city, San Nicolas, is nestled. The southern coast of Aruba is known for its perfect wind and kite surfing destinations, and the popular Baby Beach. This gorgeous coast in Aruba is much sought after for its placid waters and pristine sand beaches, making it a popular tourist hub.

While Aruba's rocky northern coast is known for its corral plateaus and tiny sandy bay openings known as Bocas, which in Papiamento translates mouths. The northern region oceans are rougher and a deeper hue of blue compared to Aruba's southern coast beaches. This is why swimming in the northern coastal beaches is not recommended.

Aruba's capital city called Oranjestad (named after the Royal House of Orange) is nestled on the western coast, featuring miles of white sand beaches, villas, all-inclusive resorts and Aruba's most popular Eagle Beach (often named as one of the planet's best beaches).

On Aruba's eastern coast lies the National Park Arikok that encompasses around 20 percent of the island's total land, while offering a staggering variety of topography and landscapes comprising caves (replete with exotic Indian drawings), sand dunes, beaches and volcanic hill formations, natural pools and other flora/fauna.

Nestled within the national park, the Jamanota hill is the island's highest point. Though the Hooibergis not Aruba's highest point, it can be viewed from any given point within the island, due to which it has earned a place on Aruba's Coat of Arms.

Aruba's rough terrain comprises some flat hills and little vegetation with zero inland water. The most striking geographical feature of Aruba is the long stretches of white sand beaches, which are the tourism (the foundation of the island's economy) mainstay.

Aruba is nestled on the Tectonic Plate along with the other ABC islands, while also being on the South American continental shelf. Therefore, it shares much of South America's topography. Aruba's terrain comprises predominantly of rock formations, especially in the island's interiors. The island's most popular rock formations are Casibari and Ayo, both of which figure prominently on every tourist must do list.

Aruba features three deep-water harbors nestled at Aruba-Oranjestad, San Nicolas and Barcadera and Oranjestad.

Garlanded by turquoise waters, Aruba's beaches are shaded stretches of white sand that offer beach bummers everything from adrenaline soaring water sports to lazy sunbathing to post-sundown bar/club hopping. The island is a popular spot for swimming, kite surfing, para-sailing, paddle boarding, snorkeling, water skiing and other action-packed adventure sports.

Aruba Wildlife

If mentioning Aruba and wildlife in the same breath conjures up images of partying away through the night on a lively beachside nightclub, bar or gambling venue (more on that later in the book) you are forgiven! However, here we are talking about the island's indigenous creatures that add to its vibrant natural profile.

Half of the lizard species existing on the planet are found in Aruba. You will find everything from cutesy iguanas to the sinister looking Caribbean dragons. Arikok National Park is a great place to spot these fascinating reptiles, along with a couple of quirky snake species. Other than the whiptail lizard, you will find a snake that defecates the moment someone picks it up. Rattlesnakes are also commonly found in the park. The island is the last remaining home of the near-extinct cascabel rattlesnake. You will also find the leaf toed Gecko only in Aruba. Other native reptiles found on the island include leatherback turtle, cat-eyed snake and more.

Donkeys are widely found mammals in Aruba, which were in fact brought to the island by Spanish immigrants. Other mammals extensively seen on the island include sheep, donkeys, cottontail rabbits, goats and more. Donkeys are spotted in large groups in Aruba's rugged regions.

Iguanas are seen darting around in search of their most preferred meal – leaves. Hiking tours are available with an experienced and expert park ranger at the Visitors Center.

Aruba has over 210 bird species including the mockingbird, yellow-headed parakeet, pelicans, orange trupial, burrowing owl, black noddies, terns and more. Many of these birds can be spotted in the early morning or late evening hours at the Bubali Ponds that was once a saltpan. Another major nesting site in Aruba is The San Nicolas Bay Keys, where plenty of native aerials can be spotted during the nesting season.

Owing to its dry and sunny climate, Aruba is home to plenty of vibrant bird species, including the prikichi (fascinatingly flamboyant. These spectacular creatures are known for their thick green plumage and flaming orange head. Blenchi birds are the tiniest bird species found in

Aruba. These vividly jewel-colored hummingbirds can be spotted flying over flowers and cacti. Look for the island's birds of prey, which include the endangered shoco (a tiny owl-like creature) and warawara.

You can't talk about wildlife in the Caribbean without referring to its thriving marine life. Aruba boasts of a rich and diverse underwater creature profile. One of the best marine adventure activities on the island is scuba diving. Get up, close and personal with seahorses, stingrays, eels, sea turtles, manta rays, clownfish, French angel, sea cucumber, butterfly fish, yellow goatfish, squirrel fish, puffers, sergeant fish and a string of other marine creatures on scuba diving adventures in the clear waters of Aruba.

While on scuba diving and marine wildlife viewing, Aruba is one of the best places on the planet for witnessing ship and airplane wrecks. This fascinating wreck diving destination has a series of Second World War remnants in addition to shipwrecks.

Local Culture

Aruba is diversified by several cultures that are reflected through everything from its fascinating multicultural history to vibrant architecture to its unique festivals.

Featuring a population of more than 110,000 people, locals here are known for their amiable disposition and zeal for hospitality. The pleasant natured locals, originating from mixed ethnic ancestries, reside and work peacefully all over the island. The typical Aruban boasts of mixed ancestry spanning European, Caquetio and African roots. Today, people from as many as 90 nations (including Europe, Peru, Haiti, Philippines and more) call Aruba home.

Despite their diverse ethnic background, Arubans share as solid national identity forged by a strong economy, education and the most enviable living standards anywhere on the Caribbean.

The region's strong economy, near perfect living conditions, and exceptional weather attract people from around the world. Many tourists have attributed their frequent visits to the island to its friendly and hospitable locals. The diverse population lends it a sort of charming variety and distinctiveness.

Language

Papiamento (local language) and Dutch are Aruba's official languages. However, most Arubans are proficient in at least four languages, including Spanish and English.

Papiamento has a distinctly friendly and informal flair that encapsulates the affability of Aruba's population. It is known to be open, unique and inclusive in nature, evident in its speech and mannerisms. The Papiamento language's origins can be traced back to the rudimentary pidgin dialect used by people speaking diverse native languages. Papiamento's base is predominantly Afro-Portuguese Creole, which went through a more complex evolution after borrowing lexicons from Spanish, Dutch, and English.

Evidence of the Papiamento language was found in 18th century Curacao official documents such as academic books and religious texts. Dutch subsidies laid their own rules of appointing Dutch language as the sole medium of imparting lessons in education institutions. Papiamento was reintroduced into Aruba's academic system fairly recently.

Religion

A majority of Aruba's residents are Catholic. However, people belonging to other religions and nationalities live in perfect harmony with the majority.

Visitors are welcome to visit all places of worship in the island.

Aruba Carnival

The legendary Aruba Carnival forms a vital component of the islands culture, festival profile,and identity. It began in 1954 as a group of small street events. It all started with a pre-Lenten festival hosted by The Tivoli Club (located in Oranjestad), the island's first private club in 1944. World War II victory of the Allied forces was marked by a momentous San Nicolas parade, comprising primarily of English/Caribbean migrants who descended upon the island to work at its oil refineries.

By 1955, several clubs came together for the earliest public Aruba Carnival. The customary Grand Parades came into existence in 1957.

Today, Aruba's grand carnival profile comprises the Lighting Parade, Pajama Party, the Grand Carnival, Children's Parades and the fancy finale – Grand Carnival Parade in Oranjestad. Among other things, you can witness the burning of King Momo's effigy on Shrove Tuesday. It is believed to represent the destruction of the carnival spirit that will emerge again in the following season.

The carnival's origins go back thousands of years when Christians feasted before giving up merriment and food/drinks during Lent. Its origins are often cited to the antiquity feasts organized to pay tribute to gods such as Saturn. Incessant colonization introduced these practices to regions of the New World, and predictably theCaribbean borrowed it from the French.

Moving Around

Aruba has a well-developed network of roads, thus offering visitors the opportunity to explore several parts of the island conveniently by road. There are many rental car firms near the airport, where travelers can hire vehicles for local sightseeing and moving around. While most roads can be accessed by regular cars, a few rugged roads require four-wheel vehicles. Motorcycle rentals are also fairly popular among tourists on the island.

Taxis are also available for commute in Aruba. Though they do not feature meters, the prices are predetermined according to government regulations. There are inexpensive and dependable bus services from major districts to main tourist hotels areas. The island's main station (bus) is housed in the heart of Oranjestad. There are companies offering charter motor facilities between Aruba's airport and tourist hotels. Look for taxis that have a "TX" on the license plate and ask to see their fare chart before or during the ride.

If you are on a budget, the best way to move around is by bus, though many visitors avoid venturing far away from their resorts, especially in the northern coast. Hire a cab to reach your hotel from the Queen Beatrix International Airport. For navigating its east coast, renting a vehicle can be a hassle-free option, depending on your budget. Similarly, if you are heading to the Arikok National Park, a rented ATV would probably be the best bet.

Since Aruba is a highly popular cruise ship port of call, there are plenty of car rental companies and cabs in and around the Oranjestad's Port Authority. Cars can be rented from the airport as well as cruise terminal, with daily rates ranging from 40 USD to 100 USD. If you are upgrading to a four-wheel drive for navigating rougher island terrains, the costs will increase.

Cruise Visitor Information

If you are arriving at the Aruba cruise terminal (as it is a highly popular port of call), the Oranjestad port has a variety of state of the art facilities across its three terminals. On arrival, visitors will be welcomes at the information booths for anything they want to know about visiting Aruba. There is an ATM kiosk right opposite the information booth along with a telecommunication desk for your communication (Wi-Fi and cellular data requirements).

Visitors can enjoy duty-free shopping inside the terminal to buy everything from quality cigars to souvenirs to fragrances. Transportation from the cruise terminal comprises tour buses, car rentals, and taxis.

Chapter 2
Aruba Attractions and Experiences

Aruba features immaculate white sand beaches, and deep sapphire waters offer plenty of sightseeing opportunities. From enjoying the rhythm of its oceanic waves to going deep sea diving (and witnessing some memorable shipwrecks) hiking through one of its verdant national parks, the island is teeming with experiences. You just can't forget the visuals of Aruba's picturesque tangerine sky at sunset or sparkling waters awash with the sun's reflection.

Here are some of the city's most sought-after (and some secret not so known insider places too) attractions, activities, and experiences.

Aruba Attractions

Eagle Beach

Eagle beach is a popular free public beach that is accessible round the clock. It is known for its hotels, villas, and timeshares in addition to a plethora of water sports activities and cruises. Equipment is available for hire and cruises can be booked in advance (check with your hotel desk). This is also the hub for chic restaurants and cafes on the island.

The beach is located in Oranjestad and is known to be a rather swish local neighborhood along with being a bustling tourist hotspot.

The beach is perfect for lazy lounging and relaxation. Plan a visit to Eagle Beach around June during the turtle hatching season. You will spot thousands of baby turtles crawling towards the ocean, an unforgettable natural phenomenon.

This is a low rise beach, which means it is geared more for sporting than swimming. If you are keen on dipping into the water to enjoy a refreshing swim, head to Palm Beach.

Another narrow, oval-shaped strip of white sand houses several resorts and hotels in Aruba's Eagle Beach neighborhood is Druif Beach. You will find a selection of eateries and rooms a few steps from the balmy Caribbean waters. Though it is located near the heart of

Oranjestad, Druif is a relaxing, calm and peaceful beach for sunbathing and mingling with locals.

Palm Beach

This high rise two-mile stretch is located on the island's western side (right next to Eagle Beach) and is pretty much the hub of Aruba's hip activities. It has ultra-glamorous resorts and swanky skyscrapers, with a sprinkling of bars, swish beachside restaurants, and boutiques. While Eagle Beach is more geared for relaxation, Palm Beach is a lively destination for revelers. Visitors can enjoy swimming and snorkeling in the balmy, high rise waters of Palm Beach.

Enjoy a stroll at sundown or indulge in a romantic, candlelight dinner barefoot on the beach. Come night, and the beach comes alive with myriad clubs, bars, and casinos. There are a couple of large shopping malls near the beach, in addition to a cinema multiplex, luxurious spas, bowling alleys and splendid fountains shows.

One of the most intriguing aspects of the beach is that the texture of the sand changes as you move from one part of the beach to another, with the mid-point believed to feature the softest sand.

The many swanky and resorts and hotels here will allow beach revelers to use their washrooms for changing. You can also buy a drink at their discounted stands or bars.

Diving enthusiasts shouldn't miss the Pedernales tanker wreck, which is a much sought after site for underwater adventure enthusiasts.

Since the entire island is a mere 20 miles in length, all popular attractions and sightseeing options are a few minutes' drive from each other. This is a free public access beach that is open throughout the day.

Baby Beach

Nestled in Seroe Colorado in southeast Aruba, Baby Beachis the archetypical Caribbean tropical paradise beach that is highly popular with families (especially those with young children). It is crescent shaped white sand stretch, featuring calm and shallow waters that make it perfect for families with kids. You can go a long distance into the water and still have your feet in at the ocean bottom.

The lagoon is also ideal for snorkeling. Head to the spot where the bay juts into the Caribbean Sea, where you will discover a vibrant smorgasbord of coral and tropical underwater creatures. Avoid venturing outside the designated snorkeling zone out of the lagoon currents are known to be overpowering.

Where there are families and kids, there are bound to be refreshment stands. You will find tons of food stands that sell delicious hamburgers and hotdogs, along with barbeque places (Big Mama's Grill is a huge hit) where you can tuck into scrumptious seafood platters and juicy grilled treats.

Free huts are set-up throughout the beach to protect visitors from the scorching sun. You' can grab beds and snorkeling gear for a rental from one of the dive rental shops on the beach. Showering facilities are also available on the beach.

Relax in a cabana on Baby Beach as you take a break from busy and touristy hotel beaches.

Renaissance Island

The ultra-luxe and chic Renaissance Island is the playground of the rich and famous who descend on Aruba's balmy shores. It exclusive resort island houses Aruba's only strip of private beaches. The 40-acre tropical paradise features crystal clear blue-green waters along with a distinctly upscale vibe. If you've seen those social media videos of pink flamingoes frolicking on the sand with guests enjoying their company, this is where it has been shot. Access to this luxury retreat is, unfortunately (or fortunately if you are a guest here) only available to guests put up at the Renaissance Aruba Resort & Casino from morning to evening. Water taxis ply every few minutes from the hotel's lobby, just behind the ocean rooms docking zone.

The beaches are a combination of adults-only and family friendly ones so check before you leave. Guests can enjoy a luxurious pampering session at the well-appointed Spa Cove or indulge in a session of tennis on the beach or feast on a scrumptious lunch menu at the Papagayo Bar and Grill, before heading back to the resort.

Pink flamingos will walk right up to visitors on the soft white sands of Renaissance Aruba Resort's private beaches, where you can feed them or offer treats. You will also spot vibrant iguanas and electric blue lizards lazily lounging on the beach.

While Iguana Beach on Renaissance Island is open to families (resort guests only), Flamingo is an adults-only Beach.

Boca Grandi Beach

Nestled on Aruba's eastern belt about 5 minutes from the heart of San Nicholas, Boca Grandi is known for its consistent trade winds, which are perfect for kite surfing. Treacherous waves and powerful currents make this and hence swimming should be absolutely avoided.

However, Boca Grandi is a beachcomber's haven with a variety of natural resources such as corals and driftwood found in large quantities here. Do not forget to take a photograph of a gorgeous beach backdrop made even more spectacular with the iconic bright and gigantic crimson anker marks at the beach entrance.

Visitors can stop here en route to Baby Beach. Catch sights of enthusiastic local surfers looping their kites over Aruba's ocean-scape.

Grape field Beach is a little known and hidden beach located adjacent to Boca Grandi. Though this secluded and peaceful beach offers near perfect surfing conditions, it is not advisable to swim or snorkel here owing to the powerful currents and winds. That does not take away from the fact that Grape field is great for families wanting to enjoy a relaxed picnic away from crowds.

Hadicurari Beach

The Hadicurari Beach or Fisherman's Huts as it is locally referred to is a rocky stretch down the Marriott Aruba Resort. Its skis are punctuated by vibrant kites and windsurfers cutting through the water. The beach was an erstwhile fishermen community, though today it has transformed into a glitzy surfing spot for water sports enthusiasts.

Hadicurari Beach is also the venue for multiple sporting events held all through the year on the island.

One of the world's and the Caribbean's largest windsurfing competition, Aruba Hi-Winds, is held during June-July at the Hadicurari Beach each year.

Malmok Beach

Malmokis a white sandy strip that is teeming with limestone formations and rugged, rocky patches. The clear blue Caribbean waters of this beach offer perfect snorkeling opportunities to visitors. Lots of catamarans and cruises boats halt right off the shore during the day to let visitors enjoy snorkeling. Expect to see a variety of reefs and shipwrecks.

The area is a popular local residential neighborhood with lavish homes and specially created windsurfing residences. Malbok Beach's main road leads to several other attractions including the iconic California Lighthouse, Arashi Beach, and an 18-hole golf, in addition to other sites. The beach becomes the hub of tourist and local activity in the morning and evening when hikers and bikers descend here for their fix of Aruba's pleasant breeze.

Rodger's Beach

This is one of Aruba's best-kept secrets (well not anymore). It is a narrow patch of white sand near the more popular Baby Beach. Rodger's is where local fishers folk anchor their fishing boats, sheltered by the bay's more composed waters. While the beach is calm during weekdays (perfect for a much-needed break from Aruba's noisier beaches), it is packed with local families on weekends.

There is a dive shop next to the beach that offers snorkeling and diving gear. You will also find shower facilities and a small restaurant adjacent to the beach.

De Palm Island

De Palm Island is accessible via a five-minute ferry trip from Aruba's mainland. It is a tiny and private patch of sand that features a plethora of activities for all-inclusive prices. Guests can enjoy everything from swimming to banana boat zipping to snorkeling.

De Palm Island's bouquet of activities also comprises several land-based recreational activities including volleyball, bingo, card games, salsa instruction sessions, beach basketball and more. Families with kids can hop over to the tiny water park, featuring waterslides and frolicking splash pools. There are other services such as massages, helmet walk and underwater Sea trek available for an additional charge.

Arashi Beach

Arashi Beach is another pleasant beach that is popular with locals and tourists for its relaxing sand huts, spacious parking lot and steady waves. The beach features composed currents and a flourishing underwater ecology, which makes it ideal for snorkeling. Arashi is nestled on the extreme northwestern tip of the island (adjacent to Boca Catalina) from where you can catch sweeping views of Aruba, including the iconic lighthouse.

Natural Pool

The Natural Pool is a sheltered natural swimming hole that is filled with water from waves crashing against rocks. Visitors can enjoy swimming and snorkeling in Aruba (which isn't very large but still pleasant). Aruba's Natural Pool is best accessed via a four-wheel drive on the island's rough roads. Hire a guide if you aren't comfortable navigating the path on your own (the roads aren't marked too well). Horse riding, hiking, and ATV tours are available throughout out the area.

Andicuri Beach

Andicuri Beach is a body boarder's manna from heaven (a few are competitions are held here). It offers a peaceful, non-touristy vibe, and is a pleasant retreat for those wanting to escape bustling crowds. Nestled on the windward coast of Aruba near the broken Natural Bridge site, the beach features striking bluffs standing next to a rugged sandy cove spot. The beach is secluded and calm and leaves you pretty much on your own.

Do not miss visiting Black Stone Beach when you are Andicuri. Though it is absolutely unsuitable for swimming (do not even think about it) and a little further down Andicuri via a dirt road, Black Stone has a gorgeous looking arch limestone bridge (yes, highly Instagrammable)

Surfside Beach

Situated in the heart of Oranjestad (adjacent to the airport), Surfside is ideal for families with young children because the water is shallow and unruffled. You can enjoy a family day out or picnic by renting beach chairs. Kitchen and bathroom facilities are available on the beach, plus there is a bar here for those looking to enjoy a drink.

Bachelor's Beach

No, you aren't going to find your hot new date (who knows though?) at the enticingly named Bachelor's Beach. However, this tiny yet pristine beach (known as Boca Tabla by locals) is a great place for beginner surfers owing to its perfect trade winds and calm waves. You will have lots of opportunities to experiment with new surfing moves in the unruffled and calm waters of Bachelor's Beach. Though there are plenty of snorkeling and deep sea diving opportunities, it isn't advisable to venture into the water without a local instructor.

Donkey Sanctuary

Located in Aruba's northeastern coast, around 8 miles from the popular Eagle Beach, Donkey Sanctuary is a non-profit outfit that is dedicated to educating and creating awareness about the caring for donkeys, which were once a main transportation mode on the island. The unwell and injured creatures receive shelter in this Santa Cruz sanctuary, where they can also interact with visitors.

Feed cups are available at the sanctuary, though you can carry your own cut apples or carrots as treats for these amiable and hard-working mammals.

The donkeys, which were once used as a means of transport, were left wandering in search food (making them susceptible to illness, injury, and abuse). Save the

Donkey foundation came up with a plan to protect and rehabilitate these creatures in a sheltered environment in 1997. Two decades later, the sanctuary moved to a larger Bringamosa location and currently houses around 130 Aruban donkeys.

Though entry is free for visitors, you are encouraged to donate an amount towards the organization's initiative of preserving and caring for the donkeys. The sanctuary is open from 9am to 4 pm. Tour facilities are available on request, in addition to a souvenir shop (the proceeds of which are diverted for fundraising).

The donkeys, with their inquisitive and endearing personalities, offer a fascinating up, close and personal encounter.

Arikok National Park

Did you know that one-fifth of Aruba is designated as a national park with a multitude of flora and fauna species gracing its landscape?

Nature enthusiasts and those bitten by the outdoor bug will enjoy exploring Aruba's popular Arikok National Park that is spread across approximately 7900 acres of land with dramatic topographical characteristics. It features a stunning cactus enveloped landscape teeming with sand dune, quirky rock formations, and caves. Then there are large boulders with intriguing Indian paintings (called Ayo). You can feast your eyes on never seen before formations of quartz, limestone, and lava.

Walk through the innumerable hiking trails (or steps) for some brilliant views and photo opportunities. Visitors also enjoy picnicking at the Natural Bridge in Anicourithat is around 7.5 meters above sea level.

The photogenic waterfront of Arikok also features the Bushiribana Ruins (ancient stone walls) that are remnants of 19th century smelting trade. Wildlife enthusiasts can spot wild goats, iguanas, a variety of snakes (and lizards) and parakeets in the park. Since roads tend to rough and treacherous, jeep tours are highly recommended if you want to go wildlife watching. Adventure struck visitors can also opt to experience the park's labyrinth of rugged hiking trails on horseback.

Park rangers preserve trails and guide visitors with information about hiking trails and personalized tours (discover the park's historical sites and wildlife). Hiking tours can be booked for a maximum of 15 people. Similarly, park ranger conducted guided tours are available for free, though it has to be booked in advance (at least a day prior).

Aruba's southeastern coast is dominated by a plethora of wildlife species, which means visitors who do not fancy finding themselves rubbing shoulders with the region's wildlife should steer clear of this region. The lush ecological belt is highly popular with wildlife enthusiasts and bird watchers (lots of migratory birds).

Spend the day exploring the caves, limestone cliffs, Amerindian art and erstwhile goldmines, in addition to observing Aruba's indigenous wildlife. The entire park is challenging to explore in a single day if you want to enjoy all experiences and sights. I'd highly recommend focusing on a couple of aspects (say wildlife and bird-watching and cave exploring) per day, and returning to other activities the following day.

Arikok National Park is not simply a park but a cluster of idyllic beaches such as the Boca Prins, Daimari Beach, and the picturesque Dos Playa. However, since the water has rough and powerful currents, swimming should be avoided here. Enjoy a dip in the island's Natural Pool.

Park admission fee is $11 per person (free for children below 17), and it is open daily from 8am to 4 pm.

Cave explorers will enjoy discovering the secluded caverns (replete with ancient paintings) at the tip of Arikok National Park. These caves are awash with stalactites, bats, and innumerable skylights. The caves offer you a unique experience of viewing Aruba's natural formations from close quarters.

Guadirkiri is the most popular cave, with two main caves interlinked with a tunnel (called the Tunnel of Love, no less). It features exquisite Arawak paintings and prints that date back several hundred years. A must do for nature and archeology buffs.

Boca Prins is an imposing coastal strip that is adorned by dramatic sand dunes and sculpted sands (formed by trade winds). At the narrow ivory sand coast of the beach, visitors can spot fascinating limestone cliffs. Swimming is not recommended here due to strong currents, but the beach is ideal for frolicking in the sand and picnicking. Hire a four-wheel vehicle if you are planning a visit to Boca Prins.

Ostrich Farm

There are tons of exciting facts you can learn about ostriches at the Aruba Ostrich Farm. Nestled in Oranjestad, the farm offers up close and personal encounters with the large birds in addition to the opportunity of learning fun facts about them from knowledgeable tour guides. Visitors will gain insights into the life of ostriches living on farms. Plus, you can enjoy feeding these friendly birds.

Visitor Tip: head to the natural bridge and goldmine remnants located in the vicinity of the park. Both are free for visitor and make for a perfect trip when combined with a visit to the Ostrich Farm.

Ostrich Farm is open daily for visitors, with tours being conducted every 30 minutes from 9 am. To 4pm. Farm tours are priced at $12/adult and $6/child. You can also make the most of your time in the Aruban Capital by combining it with a trip to one of the nearby beaches.

Butterfly Farm

Nestled at the Palm Beach opposite the Aruba Resort Hotels strip, Butterfly Farm is a lush tropical garden filled with butterfly species from all over the world. It has some of the planet's vibrant, intriguing and rare butterfly species, whose life cycle lives can be observed from the egg phase to the final butterfly phase.

Tour guides educate visitors with fun trivia and commentary on the lives of these fascinating insects. Come early in the day to witness the phenomenon of butterflies coming out from the chrysalis and embarking on their first ever flight. Do not miss the opportunities to take plenty of pictures.

A single admission ticket allows visitors a free pass to visit the park as many times as they want during their trip.

Rancho Daimari

On Aruba's northeast coast, Rancho Daimari provides exciting horseback tours of the region's surrounding attractions such as Arikok National Park, Aruba's Natural Pool and the idyllic Anducuri Beach. Visitors can also ride along the sand dunes. The ranch is built on the site of an erstwhile 17th-century coconut plantation and looks over the gorgeous Daimari Beach.

Though the path is rugged and steep, visitors of all riding abilities are allowed to enjoy the rides. Avoid if you are comfortable riding through rough and slightly slanting paths.

California Lighthouse

Initially built to warn diverting ships from Aruba's coastline, the California Lighthouse today serves as a major tourist attraction. It not only emits the warning light but also offers tourists sweeping vistas of Aruba. California Lighthouse stands as an iconic guardian of the island's northwest end in a region called Hudishibana.

On a clear, sunny day, you can catch magnificent views of the island's west coast, replete with rocky shores, rugged white sand beaches and the immaculately manicured Tierra del Sol golf course.

Go next door to the California Sand Dunes to enjoy some family fun under the sun or a romantic post-sundown stroll on the isolated coastline (plenty of privacy).

Though you can visit the lighthouse practically anytime during the day for its panoramic 360-degree views, the place is resplendent during sunset, when the sky lights up in fiery orange. Look out for the quick, green flash emitting from the lighthouse. The attraction is also open to visitors for tours at $8/person.

Dine at the adjacent restaurant - El Faro Blanco, while catching sweeping views of the Caribbean's oceanscape.

Alto Vista Chapel

The small, frills-free yet striking Alto Vista Chapel is one of Aruba's most hailed landmarks. Referred to as the Pilgrim's Church, this iconic structure was built in mid-18th century by migrant Spanish missionary Silvestre. Alto literally means highest or topmost view in Spanish. Befitting its name, the church is located atop a hill to offer stunning views of Aruba's northern shore.

Chapter 3
Aruba Activities

Aruba's varied topography, rich natural landscape and striking geographical features offer plenty of scope for outdoor activities. There are rugged beach paths, sandy dunes, action-packed hiking trails and much more. A majority of the beaches here offer perfect trade winds and temperate waves that are ideal for surfing and boarding. Aruba's thriving underwater flora and fauna (and fascinating wrecks) also offers plenty of diving and snorkeling opportunities. Being a huge outdoor and adventure activity buff, I enjoyed hiking, diving, deep sea fishing and a range of activities in Aruba.

Here are some activities that visitors can experience to make the most of their time on the hip Caribbean Island.

Deep Sea Fishing Charter Tours

Deep sea fishing charters are available at many places in Aruba, including popular ones near the Renaissance Marina. This is your best bet for deep sea fishing since the waters here are teeming with a variety of fish including game fish, barracuda, amberjack, yellow tuna, sailfish and more. Charters can be hired for half or full days with prices ranging from $220 onward for a half day charter tour and $400 onward for a full day charter.

Kayaking

Want to combine the thrill of water sports with the excitement of exploration? Consider kayaking on the balmy beaches of Aruba. You will discover lush hidden mangroves and mystical caves while enjoying vantage point views of the island from a variety of spots. Plus, who can resist the adventure of smack in the middle of crystal clear Caribbean waters? Kayaking is great for families with children aged 10 and above.

Snorkeling

Snorkeling is another popular activity in Aruba's marine-rich and balmy waters. The crystal clear waters of the island are teeming with a variety of majestic corals and tropical fish. Boca Catalina (a tiny secluded beach in the Malmok Beach region) is a popular beach for snorkelers (lots of snorkeling tours conducted here), owing to the palometas observed near the coast.

The shore is replete is sergeant and trunkfish. Venture deeper into the waters to spot colorful tropical fish and vibrant corals. The ivory sand beach can be accessed via steps, and there's plenty of parking space available.

Tres Trapi is another much sought-after snorkeling spot in Aruba, where snorkelers can find several vibrant sea stars that are not commonly found elsewhere on the island.

Malmok Beach features innumerable coves and fish that make it an ideal snorkeling spot. The beach is a hotbed for a variety of species such as trunkfish, sergeant majors, banded butterfly, French angel, trunkfish, bluehead wrasse and more. Watch out for the pointed rocks lying on the shore.

Savanetais Aruba's oldest city and its former capital. Mangel Halto, located in Savaneta, is a lesser known yet beautiful and thriving marine ecology featuring beach (perfect for snorkeling). Though it is slightly challenging to enter the beach owing to the sharp rocks, once snorkelers enter the beach they can witness the island's rich ecology including butterfly fish, blue tangs, stingrays, yellowtail snappers, parrot fishes and many more. Avoid snorkeling at Mangel Halto if you aren't a proficient swimmer because it has strong currents.

You can't talk about snorkeling without mentioning Arashi Beach in the same breath. Nestled on Aruba's northern coast, it is ideal for beginner snorkelers owing to sandy base and shallow waters. The beach is filled with large and tiny, vibrant fish species. See palometas prancing around the shore along with small bottom feeders.

Baby Beach is also good for snorkeling families. However, you need to watch out for the powerful current a little outside the bay.

Palm Island is another great Aruban snorkeling hotspot with its diverse and stunning snorkeling regions. Since the island features both shallow and deep waters, it is suitable for snorkelers of all levels. The paid snorkeling island offers everything from snorkeling instructions to gear. There is a bar on the island, where you can let your hair down after a hectic snorkeling session.

Complimentary snorkeling tours of Palm Island's reef are conducted twice a day.

Diving

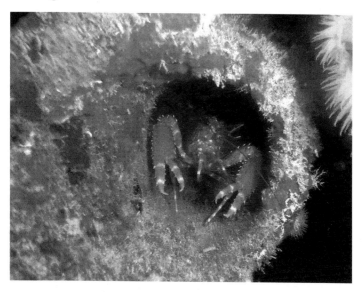

Diving on Aruba's southern coast is a peaceful and relaxing activity. The island is known all over the world for its exceptional wrecks that cater to all levels of divers. You can view everything from tugboats to fuselages airplanes to submerged vessels to large cargo ships. Nestled between Malmok and Arashi, Antilla is the island's biggest and most fascinating wreck.

Snorkelers also throng here for exploring the shallow sections of Antilla's wreck area. Other most frequented wreck centers on the island include Jane Sea (a massive concrete freighter) and Pedernales (an oil tanker). On Malmok, head towards California Lighthouse on its northern side. Antilla was an erstwhile German ship abandoned after theGerman invasion of Holland. It is a large and almost intact vessel that is known to be one of the Caribbean'smost iconic wrecks.

Divers can find a multitude of reefs lined on Aruba's leeward shore. The best diving sites in Aruba are Mas Bango Reef, Skalahein Reef, and Plonco Reef. If you fancy viewing the island's marine life without diving can hop aboard the Atlantis Submarine, where you can witness an alluring variety of marine life (while still staying dry) such as corals and shipwrecks. The Pedernaleswas also one of four large tankers defeated by a German vessel in 1942.

Since Aruba is on the lee side, the currents and sea waves are not overpowering. The northern coast of Aruba is also good though it can get a tad too rough at times. Off Aruba's southern coast, visitors can do reef diving at the popular Mangel Alto, juxtaposed between San Nicholas and Aruba's capital, Oranjestad. The region is brimming with a variety of colorful reefs and bright tropical fish.

Windsurfing and Kitesurfing

Aruba's perpetually stead trade winds have made it a highly popular windsurfing destination. Beginners to seasoned surfers enjoy sailing in the near-perfect waves of the island. It is here that the annual popular Hi-Winds Windsurfing Pro-Am Grand Prix World festival is held.

Kitesurfing is one of the island's fastest growing leisure and recreation sports. Several kiteboarding schools across Aruba conduct instructional sessions under the guidance of professional and experienced instructors.

The island boasts a perfect combination of winds, water conditions, and temperature to surfers of all levels. It is little surprise that the popular Caribbean is referred to as one of the planet's most gorgeous places to learn windsurfing. Visitors can learn surfing and rent equipment to make the most of their adventure in Aruba.

Hiking and Walking Tours

Aruba's rugged coast, national parks, sandy beaches and rocky paths are great for walking and hiking. Hiking is a great way to discover the diverse landscape and rich topography. Ensure that you shelter yourself from the scorching sun with sunblock, sunglasses, hat, a sturdy pair of hiking shoes and lots of water.

The best place for hiking in Aruba is the Arikok National Park. It covers 20 percent of the island and features more than 29 rough miles of rugged rocky trails that are perfect for exciting hikes. Maps for the hiking trails can be taken from visitor center near the entry gate for Arikok.

The most challenging is a hiking adventure is a five-hour long path winding through a rugged, rocky terrain that covers everything from cacti to rare wildlife creature sightings to desert bushes. From 620 feet, you can grab vantage point views from above Jamanota (known to be Aruba's highest point). For an unusual and thrilling adventure, consider booking a full moon nocturnal hike with an experienced naturalist.

Though you can venture out into the park on your own, it is recommended that you take a guided tour with a park ranger, who knows all paths inside out. Guide tours are complimentary. However, visitors need to book it in advance by contacting the park on +2975851234.

Landsailing

Landsailing involves moving on sand using a kart for holding sail for the required wind propulsion. The Aruban plains offer ideal conditions for land sailing. Your wind led kart is fairly tiny, light and 3 wheel mounted. Its front wheels are fixed to a mechanism that helps you steer the cart with your feet. The kart can be operated by controlling its sail, which is similar to traditional sailing through water. Aruba visitors can experience the thrill of speed in a single sailing session.

Experience upwind and downwind sailing with a slalom course for sailors of all levels. There are local land surfing schools that offer sailing instruction, equipment, and safety regulations.

Chapter 4
Insider Information and Tips

As someone who has traveled extensively throughout the Caribbean and especially Aruba, here are some insider tips and information that will help you make the most of your trip to this stunning Caribbean Island.

1. You can walk barefoot in the on the ivory sands even when the sun's heat is at its peak. The secret here is that Aruba's crushed corals and myriad shells keep the shoreline pleasantly cool. Visitors can take long walks on the island's shores throughout the day without having to worry about burning their feet. Yay! You do not have to worry about footwear.

    Having said that, the sunshine in Aruba is at its peak from 11 am to 3 pm. Ensure to apply and reapply (every two hours) to avoid sunburns and exposure to harmful ultraviolet rays. Also, it is important to maintain a healthy liquid intake to prevent dehydration. Keep taking water and lot of liquids to refuel your body. The winds here make the island's heat much more bearable.

Do not leave your hotel without your cap or hat and sunglasses.

2. When you are lost and need directions, look at the island's divi trees. No this not some unexplainable phenomenon or treasure hunt but science. The breeze originating from the island's northeast has created the indigenous tree into several artistic shapes. If you want to find your way back from Aruba's more isolated regions, follow the direction in which the divi-divitree bends and you will more often than not reach the nearest town.

3. Gambling winnings are not taxed in Aruba. Holy moly, I just saw you do a mental jig there. The next best thing after winning a fortune through gambling is not paying tax on the winning amount. You can win at a cumulative jackpot or poker; your windfalls will not be taxed here. Similarly, winnings from the government organized lottery are tax-free.

This does not mean you returning to the United States, or Canada will not alert customs. However, tourists resolve that by investing in timeshares and condominiums to return to Aruba every year. Some casinos keep their patrons' winnings in an account from which they draw money from on subsequent trips.

4. Aruba has a highly renowned film festival, where filmmakers and avid film watchers congregate to view internationally acclaimed films at the Aruba International Film Festival. Expect to rub shoulders with some Hollywood biggies and not so biggies at the hip and happening festival.

5. Come March to Novemberand visitors can witness several hundred turtle nests (some areas of the beach are made inaccessible for preserving turtle nests). Arikok National Park has tied up with The Turtugaruba Foundation for a global program to protect turtles from all over Aruba. Park rangers and foundation members monitor and protect nests, while also directing baby nests into the ocean if required. Witnessing the small hatchlings come out of their eggs, and taking their first steps in the direction of the ocean, jump into it, and take their initial swimming strokes is a sight to behold! They will sometimes swim as much as 6000 miles to reach their feeding grounds.

6. Aruba has the maximum number of sunny days in the Caribbean and the lowest rainfall in the (average of 15 inches annually), which makes it a perfect destination for those seeking sunshine. Also, since it

rests comfortably outside the hurricane belt, it rarely touches the island's shores.

7. Aruba's crime rate is very low, making it the Caribbean's safest destination. However, visitors should still be vigilant and use their common sense. Avoid hanging out in dark, isolated beach stretches or alleys post-sundown. Overall though, tourists do not have to worry about safety and crime.

8. Few people know about Aruba's harvest festival, locally referred to as the burying rooster festival. A rooster is buried underground, with its head protruding out. Then the locals get together and dance together (dressed in vibrant colors). People are blindfolded and decapitate the bird one at a time. However, the ritual has become more compassionate off late, and they use a dummy bird or flag instead of a real one.

9. Iguana meat is a local delicacy here in Aruba. Its taste is similar to chicken, and foodies may want to try it! Several local eateries offer iguana based preparations around the island.

10. If you are on a budget and looking for low-priced accommodation options, skip the private beaches and all-inclusive resorts and head to one of the stone beach homes that are rented to tourists for around $30/weekend. The houses are nothing fancy. Sometimes they are without basic amenities such as

water and electricity while being scenic and peaceful all the same. Aruba's beaches cannot be purchased. However, those who already have them are permitted to keep them.

11. Some tourists stack rocks on top of each other at the wishing garden. However, locals are trying to get people to stop this practice since it is known to create an obstacle in the flow of water and disrupts the region's ecology.

12. Those wanting to witness remnants of Aruba's 19th century gold rush should head to Bushiribana Gold Mills for its charming old buildings.

13. While several Caribbean island's treat homosexuality as an unlawful and punishable offense, Aruba is relaxed and gay-friendly. Nonstraight folks are welcome to get their pride here for an enjoyable vacation, unlike several other skeptical Caribbean destinations. Aruba is more South American than the Caribbean since it is a mere 18 miles from Venezuela.

14. Tourists need not spend on bottled water in Aruba. The pleasant sunshine island has its distillery, situated in Balashi. Here seawater is transformed into drinking water. Arubans are proud of this water and often refer to it as the world's best water. When you hear a local ask for Balashi Cocktail, all they want is water.

On the subject of drinks, Arubans are also huge champagne fans. They love to experiment with their bubblies, and enjoy combining it with fruits, juices, and sorbets to create lip-smacking concoctions. You can't miss their Champagne mojito for anything!

15. Though this information should be cross-checked with cpb.gov and cbsa-asfc-gc.ca (as it can keep changing), Aruba offers visitors from the United States of America and Canada a duty-freeexemption of $800.00 per visitor. Duty-free shops at the airport ensure that visitors do not end up paying large taxes and import duties on goods.

You will find lots of shopping strips lined with shops. Plus there are swanky malls and unusual boutiques brimming with local fashion. Do not skip visiting the myriad city emporiums filled with chic yet traditional silver and diamond jewelry.

Other things that can be picked up in Aruba include watches, fragrances, trendy resort wear, fashion accessories, electronics, linens, lingerie, swimwear, designer apparel, souvenirs, and artifacts. Plus, there are shopping centers housing eateries, theatres, and nocturnal entertainment options on the busy Palm Beach strip.

16. Keep in mind that it isn't considered good etiquette to sports swimwear anywhere else other than by the beach or pool. Also, even though this may seem

basic, always seek permission before photographing people.

17. Men should ideally sport dress shorts or slacks for dinner since denim pants are not permitted in most restaurants. Ensure to pack proper formal slacks and shorts if you plan to dine in swish restaurants.

Chapter 5
Oranjestad

Aruba is known all over the world for its ivory beaches, trade winds, isolated caves and a plethora of activities including windsurfing, skydiving, jet skiing, parasailing, fishing, scuba diving, and cruising. From playing golf to riding a horse to hiking in national parks to taking guided bus tours, there's a lot to do here.

It isn't all beaches and sunshine here. However, each Aruban city has its own character that is evident in its colonial remnants, shopping centers, old city structures and churches. Here are some ideas for making the most of your time in Aruba's old-worldly yet emerging, trendy cities.

Oranjestad

Oranjestad is Aruba's charming capital city known for its bustling cruise ports, colorful buildings (pastel-hued) and a quintessentially laidback Spanish-Caribbean vibe that rests alongside clean streets, where visitors can find plenty of art galleries, restaurants, entertainment venues, museums, shops, and waterfronts.

Visitors can access the immaculately maintained Wilhelmina Park, one of Oranjestad's popular tourist draws, especially from June to October, when the flora is blooming at its fullest. The attraction was originally created as a lighthouse and vantage point for viewing Aruba's scenic surroundings. There are plenty of attractions here including King William III Tower (Fort Zoutman), Aruba Historic Museum (featuring artifacts about Aruba's history) and more.

Other city highlights are National Archeological Museum, Butterfly Farm, harbor market, Access Art Gallery and Numismatic Museum, with currency going back several thousand years. The city is a nice place for strolling and soaking up an old-worldly atmosphere on cobbled streets.

Climate

The average temperature of Oranjestad is 28 degrees Celsius. Weather here remains fairly temperate throughout the year with bright, clear skies on most days. With a pleasant and near-perfect weather, visitors do not have to worry about rainfall. The city has its share of cloudy days, though on most days it only drizzles early morning or late evening. The remaining days are replete with sunshine.

For example, the average rainfall per month is 60-70 millimeters a month. The sunny and gorgeous tropical Oranjestad weather is a huge draw for tourists from all over the world.

Moving Around

Moving around in the downtown region on a bike is easy on a pleasant, windy day since it's all bright and sunny. When the heat is too harsh, take a cab, which will not come to more than USD 8-15 throughout the city. Taxis are almost always available just outside popular tourist hotels and resorts.

It is an easy and affordable way to experience Oranjestad, especially if you aren't familiar with the city. Since English is widely spoken and understood throughout the city along with a bunch of other languages such as Spanish and the local Papiamento, you will not have a tough time reading signs or navigating places.

Fun Things to Do

Oranjestad is an enjoyable destination, where visitors can enjoy several activities such as fishing, boat riding, snorkeling, and parasailing.

Shopping for jewelry and keepsakes is popular in the markets of Oranjestad. Jewelry prices are much lower than those in North America owing to the myriad jewelry shops. You will find some great bargains on diamonds, pearls, and precious metals. Your purchases will have a higher value back home in the United States than the rates at which you bought them.

However, despite all attractions and sightseeing options, the primary draw of Oranjestad is its family-friendly ivory beaches.

Aruba's capital city plays host to several events and festivals throughout the year, including the Annual Carnival Celebration, Bon Bini Festival, Soul Beach Music Festival (a three night long outdoor party and concert that hosts reggae artists from all over the Caribbean), Touch Parade and Children's Grand Carnival Parade.

Safety

Much like the rest of Aruba, Oranjestad is a fairly low-crime and safe city though this does not rule out the chances of crime by fellow travelers/tourists. This means you have to exercise common sense and avoid venturing out alone in secluded alleys after sunset. Also, do not venture too far from your hotel, especially if you plan to spend the evenings drinking.

One of the best parts of the city is that locals never pressurize or coerce tourists into buying things from their shops. Also, visitors are not bothered by panhandlers and homeless seeking money. On the whole, the crime rate is low, and there's nothing to stress about here as far as crime is concerned.

Eating Out

7 West Bar and Restaurant

Located right off the bustling Oranjestad Harbor, 7 West Bar Restaurant is a nice place to enjoy scenic harbor vistas (complete with docked boats) of the Caribbean waters. 7 West is known acclaimed for its affordable gourmet menu that has both tourists and locals thronging here. Tuck into their special lunch platter here, which generally features a fresh catch of the day.

Café the Plaza

Founded by Dutch immigrants more than two decades ago, Café the Plaza is a sort of local institution. It is located smack in the middle of the city's Renaissance Marketplace and is the perfect venue for a lazy meal after a hectic shopping session around town. The eatery is pretty accommodating of special requests and serves everything from pancakes to sandwiches throughout the day. Grab their on the go yet delicious sandwich for a hurried lunch.

Cuba's Cookin

Savor a slice of Cuba in Oranjestad with another Renaissance Marketplace located restaurant – Cuba's Cookin. The place brims with authentic Cuban charm right down to its décor, music, and menu. Owner Markus has infused the place to an unmistakable Havana 60's bar vibe borrowed from his travels to Cuba for the last 15 years. Do not leave without trying their scrumptious Cuban specialties such as ropavieja (braised steak) or pollo con ace tunas (a chicken and olives preparation), washed down with the popular mojito.

El Gaucho Argentine Grill

Housed in a restored, erstwhile colonial house, this is Aruba's first Argentine eatery way back in 1977. Going from strength to strength today is a highly recommended name for steaks on the island. El Gaucho is known to whip up a mean selection of traditional Argentinean grilled treats. There is a special menu for those craving local Caribbean food too. Its specialties? Shish kabob, grilled beef tenderloin skewer, and chorizo.

Wilhelmina

This may not be as old as the other restaurants on this list, but Wilhelmina has quickly made a name in Aruba's culinary profile owing to its epicurean cuisine inspired by ingredients and flavors from around the world. The menu indicates every dish with a tiny flag. And yes, bouillabaisse and roasted peking duck happy co-exist alongside each other on Wilhelmina's varied menu.

Arubaville

Located on the Oranjestad's outskirts, Aruba Ville has a well-appointed yet relaxed waterfront ambiance at Laguna Bay. It is not just a single restaurant,but a full-fledged dining village comprising multiple lounges, a game center for groups (perfect for families), lazy hammocks, a dining room and more Go for dinner and enjoy their fresh seafood. Though the menu is largely global, the vibe is distinctly Caribbean.

CILO City Lounge

CILO City Lounge is an all-day eatery, located in the popular Renaissance Marketplace area.You have to sample the restaurant's city breakfast spreads. New York, for instance, features bacon, a couple of scrambled eggs, yogurt, sausages, fruit, toast, and jelly. Enjoy vistas of the buzzing marina from CILO's rooftop. They have a happy hour in the evenings when you can clink glasses of half-priced drinks with friends. Cheers!

The West Deck

Looking into the azure waters of the Caribbean towards the island's northern windward side, the restaurant is a bustling, relaxed and family-friendly dining venue that is much recommended by both locals and tourists. You can tuck into everything from fresh cut fish to local sauces (the lip-smackingmahi-mahi or chili calamari). The al fresco décor and stunning harbor views are some other reasons to dine at The West Deck.

Yemanja Woodfire Grill

This Renaissance Hotel located restaurant is known for its uber-hip factor and fusion Caribbean delicacies. If you are homesick for some good old European grub yet want to sample local flavors, look no further than

Yemanja. Its wood fire is traditionally operated by food sourced from Aruba. The best part- the staff is more than happy to cater to special dietary restrictions (yay vegan and gluten-free), something many restaurants in town do not offer.

Gelastissimo Bistro

Situated in the heart of Oranjestad, Gelastissimo is a relaxed and refreshing restaurant, known for its authentic Dutch colonial type structure and unusual Italian menu. The old worldly charm featuring bistro serves a nice range of pizzas and paninis at reasonable prices. Grab one their salads for a quick and delicious lunch. Do not miss their signature gelatos, sorbets made from fresh, Aruba grown fruits.

Driftwood

Located in downtown Oranjestad, Driftwood is where you can enjoy the quintessential oversized lobsters, gigantic shrimp and other succulent fresh seafood that you see in travel magazines and brochures. Their menu comprises local flavors served in a rustic looking driftwood dining space. Try their authentic Aruban preparations such as filet of fish (with creole sauce), starfish broth – all served with the island's traditional cornbread called pan bati. Even something as basic and steamed vegetables and potato preparation of choice will be infused with stunning local flavors.

Gostoso

Gostoso is another fusion Caribbean-Portuguese restaurant that is ideal for a casual dining at affordable prices. The food is known to be scrumptious, while the atmosphere is relaxed and cozy. If a pocket-friendly, local neighborhood restaurant is on your mind, look no further than Gostoso.

Iguana Joes

The quirkily named Iguana Joes is one of the island's most recommended and hailed restaurants for fresh and authentic Caribbean preparations. The menu features a fine selection of local treats such as chicken enchiladas, coconut flavored shrimp, mahi-mahi, roasted chicken, and the highly popular grass-fed filet mignon. Try their delectable jerk chicken on skewers or decadent chicken nachos (dripping with cheese, guacamole, and sour cream).

Pinchos Bar and Grill

One of Aruba's must do (and finest) dining experiences is at the ultra-romantic Pinchos Bar and Grill. Who can resist catching stunning sunset and ocean vistas from a charming wooden seating deck, while tucking into a range of international flavors? Pinchos is a local institution known for its American-Caribbean and special dietary restrictions menu. Wash down authentic island preparations with a cocktail at sundown, while viewing the tangerine ocean sky lit up at sunset.

Where to Stay

Aruba's capital Oranjestad offers a mix of accommodation options ranging from intimate boutique hotels to all-inclusive hotels to swish private island resorts. It has a good mix of properties ideal of different types of visitors and budgets. Travelers of all budgets can enjoy a slice of Oranjestad's vibrant colonial streets, and its surrounding attractions by putting up at one of these places.

Here's a list of some of Oranjestad'swell-known hotels.

Renaissance Aruba Resort and Casino

You can't talk about hotels in Oranjestad without mentioning the ultra-swish and luxe Renaissance Aruba Resort and Casino. This property is nothing short of a tropical paradise with its private island, a variety of beaches (40 acres to be precise) and a bouquet of well-appointed amenities. In addition to a full-service spa, the resort also features a well-equipped fitness center and a relaxing pool.

Insider tip: If your budget permits, opt for their marvelous views offering Ocean King room that offers gorgeous bay vistas. Do not miss a visit to the adults-only Flamingo Island or the family-friendly Iguana Island.

Wonders Boutique Hotel

This is a small and intimate boutique hotel that spells relaxation and elegance. You will enjoy the privacy and hominess of a B & B with the exceptional service and vibe of a five-star hotel. This is an adults-only property that emphasizes on offering personalized service. You can opt to enjoy breakfast in bed and other such special requests.

Talk of the Town Hotel and Beach Club

Talk of the Town is a three-star property that is known to be fully booked almost all the time. It is known for its affordable tariff, convenient location, comfortable rooms, and lovely pool/sun courtyard. The palm sprinkled courtyard (replete with underwater seats, hot tubs, and sun decks)is a pleasant space for relaxing with the family. The Surfside Beach is a hop's distance from the property.

Divi Village Golf and Beach Resort

The Divi Village Golf and Beach Resort feature everything from pleasant rooms to attentive staff to lush, well-maintained grounds. Plus, they'll ferry you in a cart to other casinos, resorts and other nearby places. There are lots of family-friendly pools. The drinks here are known to be lip-smackingly good and affordable.

Try their half off happy hour specials during evenings or enjoy grilled treats on the resort's popular viewing deck. Unlike many other places, the staff is courteous and always eager to help you have a good time, even when you aren't dining with them or looking for dining options in the vicinity. That is a huge bonus for me!

Bucuti and Tara Beach Resort

Bucuti and Tara Beach Resort is an adults-only property nestled on 14 acres of the island's western tip. The boutique hotel features 104 guest rooms (that offer complete privacy and intimacy) with private balconies and solar-powered showers. Guests can catch sumptuous views of the adjoining Eagle Beach while enjoying Bucuti's languid surroundings. While it is priced on the higher end of the spectrum, the property comes with its shares of bells and whistles, including an uber-romantic dining experience in a private beach cabana.

Costa Linda Beach Resort

Nestled on Aruba's northwestern strip, Costa Linda is conveniently situated in the vicinity of several island attractions, including a bunch of casinos and the popular Eagle Beach. The beach resort features a variety of apartment-style suites equipped with kitchens, private balconies, and lazy sitting areas. Plus, there is a huge pool along with several tennis courts, a well-appointed spa/salon and lounge chairs (with a backdrop of lush palm trees).

You can just hop over into the Caribbean's turquoise waters owing to Costa Linda's easily accessible location. Guests can participate in several activities including salsa instructions, yoga sessions, pool games, karaoke, arts and more. Their multiple in-house restaurants serve everything from authentic Caribbean steaks to quick-fix pizzas.

Amsterdam Manor Beach Resort

The quintessential Dutch architecture of Amsterdam Manor Beach Resort and Spa features colonial style yellow-red walls and roofs that stand out charmingly among the Oranjestad's towering buildings. The rooms are functional and basic at best. However, it is Amsterdam Manor's intimate and attentive service that wins the day! All their rooms feature a complete kitchenette along with a private terrace and complimentary Wi-Fi.

Guests can enjoy cocktails from the rooftop bar while enjoying views of the palm-studded shore. If you fancy tucking into fresh seafood smack in the middle of the sand, they've got you covered with Passions on the

Beach restaurant. Palm Beach's glitzy casinos and clubs are a 15-minute drive away from the property.

Manchebo Beach Resort & Spa

Enter one of Manchebo Beach Resort & Spa's rooms, and the first thing you will notice is its pleasant walk0in showers and private balconies (with lovely views). This is no bells and whistles, fuss-free property located on the idyllic shores of Eagle Beach. Though may not be as swish as other properties in the vicinity, Manchebo is peaceful and affordable. It features 72 basic yet spacious and neatly appointed rooms facing the sea and garden. There is a relaxing pool and free beach cabanas.

Guests can also book a relaxing treatment at the resort's outdoor massage cabin or participate in a complimentary yoga session. The resort has a fine selection of eateries, the most popular being its Mediterranean-Caribbean menu at Ike's Bistro.

Chapter 6
Noord

Noord is an Aruban town located in its Tanki Leendert administrative unit and featured a population of 16, 944 people in 2000. Currently, it is one of the island's most populous towns that is known for its high rise resorts, swish restaurants, sun-swept beaches, shopping malls and the iconic California Lighthouse. It is here that the Alto Vista Chapel is housed. It is popular as the birthplace of Major League pitcher Sidney Ponson.

Top Things to Do in Noord

There is a family-friendly beach at Noord that is known to be serene and relaxing. The beach is also home to several swish resorts and hotels, where you can enjoy luxury on the idyllic Caribbean shores.

Plenty of local tour organizers (Aruba Adventures) organize sea and land-based adventure activities including snorkeling and sailing. Party boats can also be hired for viewing Aruba's crystal clear waters up, close and personal.

Visit the Rancho La Ponderosa, a pleasant ranch with lots of exciting hiking trails and well-bred horses.

Noord hosts a highly popular annual Children's Carnival Parade that is organized during February.

Witness the Santa Ana Roman Catholic Church that was erected in 1776, and symbolized one of the region's most eminent religious meeting venues along with Alto Vista Chapel. The church has been restored multiple times during the past last couple of centuries. Do not miss the neo-gothic, hand-carvedoak altar.

Visit the Philips Animal Garden (nice for families), which is a non-profit center that works towards the care and rehabilitation of a variety of animal species (funded by tours and donations). It is a small farm, where you can enjoy feeding rescued creatures (the ostrich eats out of your palm). There is a cute little Shetland pony that chases farm visitors. You can enjoy sitting on one of the park's shaded benches in a charmingly rustic backdrop. A small visitor admission fee goes towards the welfare and care of these creatures.

Where to Eat

Here is a list of some of the best places for visitors to dine in Noord

2 Fools and A Bull

Patrons swear by the no-bulls food and courteous service (by owners Bas and Pauly) at this Palm Beach located eatery. The food is high in flavor, with each course getting even better than the previous. They also have a fine selection of wine and desserts (handmade by

Bas). Not surprising that customers keep coming back for more.

Wacky Wahoo's

This is a tiny Palm Beach, Noord restaurant that is known for its fresh seafood preparations. It's tough to get a table here, so it is recommended that you make reservations ahead (at least a couple of weeks to a month ahead, yes it is that popular).

Without a reservation, you may have to wait in queue for a table. If you crave fresh and delicious Caribbean entrees at affordable prices in Noord, this is your place. Lookout for their daily specials and chef's special menu.

Anna-Maria's Autentico Ristorante Italiano

One of Noord's best-kept dining secrets (I do not blame the locals), Anna-Maria's Autentico Ristorante Italiano, another quaint little family-owned eatery known for its utterly scrumptious Italian treats. You will not just be warmly welcomed and seated by the owners. They'll also ensure that you enjoy the finest and most authentic Italian meal whipped up using fresh local ingredients.

This no-fuss backyard eatery serves some of the most tempting Italian fare, including a delicious burrata appetizer, pasta, and fresh seafood. The portions are generous and the prices, reasonable.

Bavaria German Restaurant

If you are put at one of the Palm beach resorts property and crave inexpensive German beer and cuisine, Bavaria may be a good bet. They have an extensive beer menu to keep you cool in Aruba's warm weather. Plus there are tons of scrumptious food treats, including chicken schnitzel, cheese soup, sausages, generously sized potato pancakes (served with a traditional accompaniment of applesauce) and more.

The Kitchen Table By White

You can't leave Noord without trying The Kitchen Table By White's tasting dinner menu Start by sipping on a refreshing glass of bubbly in the hypnotic backdrop of the Caribbean. With amazing wine pairings for each course, you will also enjoy watching chefs painstakingly prepare every item (and even offer you details about each dish). The presentation is flawless,and so is the taste.

Where to Stay in Noord

Divi Aruba Phoenix Beach Resort

Juxtaposed between the verdant Bubali Bird Sanctuary and the white sand Palm Beach, Divi Aruba Phoenix Beach Resort is surrounded by a formation of natural pools. Every room is equipped with a well-equipped kitchen along with a private terrace and microwave. Enjoy an open dining experience at Divi's Pureocean restaurant.

Guests love the easy access to Palm Beach. There is a free shuttle service to The Links at Divi Aruba Golf Course and the Alhambra Casino, located at a short distance from the resort. Note that its in-house bars shut at around 10 pm, which can be a disappointment for some guests.

Chapter 7
San Nicholas

San Nicolas is befittingly referred to as Aruba's "Sunrise City." It is situated twelve miles to the southeast of the island's capital city, Oranjestad. The quiet and idyllic coastal town is known for its charming, colonial-era promenade Zeppenfeldstraat, a handful of shops, some restaurants/bars, a small art gallery and architecturally fascinating buildings. A cluster of refineries dominates San Nicholas' landscape since it was one of the most prominent erstwhile hubs during the spice and oil trade heydays.

Visitors looking to enjoy the sunshine, food and laidback vibe of the Caribbean will not be disappointed by San Nicholas. In contrast to Palm Beach's swanky resorts and high rises, the town radiates a more relaxed, no-fuss and untouristy feel. This does not, however, make it uninteresting and inspiring. It comes alive with some exuberant music and carnivals (brought to the island by migratory workers from the English Islands and Trinidad).

Though San Nicholas is Dutch administered, a majority of its residents originate from a Caribbean-British lineage, with English as their first language. If there's one thing that is quintessentially San Nicholas, it is the town's steel pan music, the planet's most recent acoustic instrument.

Bear in mind that Saint Nicholas is a predominantly working man's town and therefore more low-key and affordable than many of the other islands other high priced regions. If you want to get away from the crowds and enjoy Aruba's fine weather and food at affordable prices, you may want to check it out. However, do not expect the same infrastructure, public transport facilities, and amenities that you find in Aruba's more touristy cities such as Oranjestad and Noord.

Things to Do

Come Thursdays and visitors can participate in the Carubbian Festival, a vibrant and lively carnival celebrating Aruba's spirit of fun and festivity. There's lots of music, crafts, authentic, homemade local treats and live shows.

You can't miss San Nicholas' calm waters and pristine sandy shores at Rodger's Beach and the family-friendly Baby Beach. Boca Grandi is great for kite-surfing.

Where to Eat

Charlie's Restaurant & Bar

Visit Charlie's Restaurant & Bar on the way to Baby Beach. It isn't easily visible but more than worth it when you manage to grab a table here. The décor is Tropical Island funky (with an assortment of cool accessories hanging from walls). Charlie's features a welcoming and laidback atmosphere, with amazing food thrown in for good measure. Sample their baby back ribs (served with a delicious and unusual sauce). When the sauces get too fiery to handle, do some chilled beer firefighting.

The drive bar style place featuring vibrant memorabilia from all over the island also has an amazing seafood lunch menu. You may want to try the highly recommended shrimp platter, lamb chops, and flavor some fish soup.

Charlie's has been much sought after right from the time scuba divers began their underwater expeditions in the mid-20th century. The treasures they unearth from the ocean grace the ceiling and walls of the bar, which makes it a sort of diver's museum built over several decades.

Kamini's Kitchen

Another frills-free dining option that is known for its authentic Caribbean preparations, including goat curry (do not forget to ask for their signature hot sauce for more flavor), bami chicken curry and more. Try their bami and grouper combinations, which are known to be a local favorite. If you want to tuck into something local and authentic, while still being kind to your pocket, Kamini's wins the day!

The Rum Reef Bar and Grill

Another culinary stop when you visit Baby Beach, The Rum Reef Bar and Grill is a nice place for enjoying some refreshing tropical drinks and sandwiches. You will want to try their scrumptious crab salad sandwich (their wings and fries are also good) and the popular pink paradise cocktail. The restaurant is a good option for those looking to grab a drink and quick bites while returning from the beach.

Big Mamma Grill Bar

This Baby Beach located restaurant is known for its delicious grouper sandwiches with sides of fries. Enjoy a round of fast food while catching sweeping ocean views from your table. However, be prepared for a long wait when the restaurant is crowded during peak meal hours. The shrimps are tasty, and BIG Mamma also features a fine selection of drinks.

Baby Beach Shack

Located in the vicinity of Big Mamma Grill, this is a lot more low key than the former. You can grab beer and ice-cream for $3 each. The menu consists of typical shack items such as fried finger food and chilled drinks. Baby Beach's service can get slower during peak hours, and unlike other places, there are no restrooms here.

A shrimp sandwich as Baby Beach Shack will set you back by $15, while a cheeseburger comes for $4 (you can pick your fillings). They also have a nice selection of drinks and catchy Bob Marley tunes blasting from the stereo. Reasonably priced fast food with a stunning ocean view, what more do you want?

Tortuga Beach Bar

Tortuga Beach Bar is frequented by kite surfers due to its convenient Boca Grand venue. It is literally a one-man show since the Peter, the owner handles pretty much everything from cooking to serving to bartending himself (and still manages to retain his exuberance and warm spirit). He also has a talent for selecting good music to play at the bar. Located smack in the middle of the beach, Tortuga is great for grabbing a cold beer and finer food.

Tuck into their delicious and hearty cheeseburgers, while witnessing the beach's thrilling kitesurfing activities. A nice place for relaxing, chilling out and getting to know more about kitesurfing.

The New Pueblito Paisa

This small yet authentic Colombian restaurant is known for its generous portions, small prices and warm ambiance. The food is made using fresh local ingredients and worth the sometimes long wait. Peublito Paisa is easy to find (at Helfrichstraat 40) and wheelchair accessible. Come early since the place gets crowded during peak lunch and dinner hours.

Where to Stay

Aruba Beachfront Home in the Colony

Nestled in a quiet and unruffled San Nicolas neighborhood, this vacation rental home is about 25 minutes ride from the Queen Beatrix International Airport. It a hop away from the beach and offers complimentary Wi-Fi, among other basic amenities. The property is ideal for those looking to live near the beach and discover nearby attractions such as Juwana Morto and the family-friendly, Palm Island.

Astoria Hotel and Restaurant

This is an inexpensive, frills-free property that is preferred by honeymooners for its convenient location (a mere 5 to 10-minute walk from most activities). The hotel also has a relaxing pool and is perfect for those seeking fun under the sun on a budget. It isn't anything fancy mind you, just a couple of rooms located above a restaurant, which means it good if you are looking for a budget stay that is still within easy reach of most town attractions.

Chapter 8
Palm Beach

Aruba's two-mile-long stretch is known as the Palm Beach. It is more a tourist-centric district than a city, which is known for its swish high rise resorts, water sports, hip beach bars, shops and calm waters (ideal for swimmers and snorkelers). Take a walk down this glamorous strip at dawn or sunset to enjoy a view of the sparkly Caribbean waters. Visitors can enjoy everything from romantic candlelight dinner smack in the middle of the beach to lazy sunbathing throughout the day.

Come sunset, and the trendy touristy area comes alive with a glittering line-up of noisy clubs, bars, and casinos. Facilities here include shopping, bowling, spas, water fountain displays and much more. If you want to be where the action is, head to the ultra-lively Palm Beach.

Top Palm Beach Experiences

Go on a memorable sunset catamaran cruise on a luxury catamaran to enjoy breathtaking views of not just Palm Beach but other parts of Aruba's azure coastline. These cruises often feature lots of native music, narration, and dancing. Enjoy tropical cocktails as you watch the sun melting into the horizon. Many tour operators offer complimentary snacks on these tours.

Enjoy parasailing over the balmy waters and white coast of Palm Beach during a 10-20 minute session with expert guidance and instruction from experienced parasailing professionals. There are many tour operators conducting parasailing tours on Palm Beach. Do not forget to carry your camera for some awesome photo opportunities.

Diving is another popular activity on the island, what with its rich reefs, iconic wrecks and a large variety of tropical fish. Look out for butterfly fish as you negotiate the sultry, blue Caribbean waters. The unspoiled marine treasures in the sea here include eels and shelters rays, making for an utterly scenic adventure.

Where to Eat

Aqua Grill

With Aruba comfortably wearing the crown of the Caribbean's food capital, it's no surprise that it has restaurants such as Aqua Grill. This one stands out as a swish seafood food venue that is popular for its fresh seafood (believed to be flown in from different parts of the world). It has a distinctly upscale ambiance and also offers a nice non-seafood menu. They also have a large wine selection, along with food that is immaculately presented and tastes equally good.

Blossoms

This well-appointed Japanese and Chinese restaurant offer a range of eastern delicacies, including sushi and teppanyaki. The rich and authentic flavors are created using fresh local ingredients.

Atardi

This is another well-kept island secret (not anymore though). Marriott's oceanfront restaurant offers the perfect backdrop for an ultra-romantic, post-sunset meal (with vistas of the ocean and sunset). Atardi in the local language Papiamento means late afternoon, and sure enough, late afternoons are best spent here. Though this is primarily a seafood restaurant, other meats are also available.

Try their delectable seafood preparations such as Lobster Tail, Sea Bass in a choice of flavors. You will also get chicken breast and the very popular filet mignon. All in all, if you want to savor fresh seafood in anuber cool seafront ambiance, Atardi is your place!

Where to Stay

The Ritz Carlton

Nestled on Aruba's northwest coast, the Ritz Carlton does full justice to the brand's signature hype in terms of service, amenities, and location. You will start your day with the trimmings of a refreshing welcome drink, followed by plenty of frills including unique spa treatments (on a well-appointed 15,000 spa premises), casino table games, and kids club (to keep your little one engaged with a range of board games and craft activities).

Guests can also indulge in lazy swimming sessions are the sprawling pool or opt for more daredevil activities such as snorkeling, sailing and paddle boarding.

Hyatt Regency Aruba Resort Spa & Casino

Sitting pretty on the ivory sands of Palm Beach, this glitzy five-star property offers a host of luxury packages and amenities, true to the renowned Hyatt chain of hotels. Every one of its 357 rooms features a large LCD television, a cool iHome radio clock, and the popular massive Hyatt beds. There's a Camp Hyatt Watapana for children, while parents can enjoy pampering sessions at the in-house Zoia Spa. There is a multi-level pool, complete with a waterfall along with beach basketball and a charming, thatched beach cabana.

Guests can choose from 10 in-house restaurants and bars, including an exclusive 'on the beach' dinner service. Book during low tourist seasons since prices tend to be much lower and you will find an empty beach cabana to relax (tough during peak tourist season).

Hilton Aruba Caribbean Resort & Casino

This former Radisson property was taken over by Hilton in 2015. The upgraded and renovated property today comprises sprawling guestrooms in addition to two huge swimming pools, five in-house dining options and rooms featuring private patios, complimentary Wi-Fi, and luxurious baths.

Enjoy a massage at Hilton's oceanfront spa or let your little ones let their hair down at the Kid's Club Room (a supervised activity area).

Hotel Riu Palace Aruba

This is another lovely Palm Beach located property that is known for its comfortably appointed rooms and scenic views. Hotel Riu Palace features 450 guestrooms with hydro-massage bathtubs, no less. At a flat room booking price, you can also avail the hotel's buffets meals (breakfast, lunch, and dinner). Guests can relax at the property's swimming pools or sunbathe on the adjoining beach.

Occidental Grand Aruba Resort

A part of the Occidental Hotels stable, this popular all-inclusive resort is located on the island's northwestern belt. Each of Occidental Grand Aruba Resort's 380 rooms features a private terrace, along with a paid Wi-Fi service and a luxuriously appointed vibe. The resort's Premium Jacuzzi Ocean facing rooms have relaxing Jacuzzis offering spectacular ocean views (heavenly!).

Chill on a chaise lounge near the pool or soak up some sunshine at the beach downstairs. Guests can enjoy a host of activities such as tennis or an action-packed kayaking adventure. The property boasts of seven in-house restaurants and bars including El Olivado and the buffet restaurant, The Palm.

Conclusion

Again, thank you for purchasing my book Aruba – The Official Travel Guide.

I sincerely hope this book was able to offer you all the information you need to make the most of your time on this lovely Caribbean Island. I've included lots of little-known insider tips and information that will help you make your vacation even more memorable. From the best places to eat to the most popular attractions and activities to the best hotels and resorts, I've tried to include as much valuable information as possible on enjoying your trip as a first timer to Aruba.

The next step is to simply book your tickets (if you haven't already) to Aruba and use all the tips mentioned in this one-stop Aruba information resource.

Finally, if you truly enjoyed this book and found it useful, please share your thoughts by writing a review on Amazon. It'd be highly appreciated.

Here's to your exciting, fun-filled and unforgettable Aruban adventure!

Book Description

Want to know Aruba inside-out even though you haven't stepped on the island yet?

Want to know all the little known, insider tips and information that locals do not want you to know?

Want to enjoy the best of Aruba's attractions and activities?

You will find all this and much much more on the pages of this exclusive and one of its kind Aruba travel guide to help you make the most of time on this sunshine, ivory sand and turquoise water Caribbean Island.

From the best places to eat at in Oranjestad to combing through the little known (and thankfully uncrowded) beaches of Aruba, I've got it all covered.

Here are some things covered in the book

- Local events and festivals that visitors can participate in

- Best places to eat at and stay in various Aruban cities and tourist strips

- Secret tips for making the most of your visit to local attractions

- In-depth information about local culture and way of life

- A comprehensive guide to the island's beaches and which beaches you should visit based on your preferences and objectives

And much more.

If you are looking to save time and money, while making the most of your time under the Caribbean sun, look no further. This is the guide for you.

92803632R00059

Made in the USA
Columbia, SC
30 March 2018